LEON

Brownies, Bars & Muffins

NATURALLY FAST RECIPES

LEON

Brownies, Bars & Muffins

NATURALLY FAST RECIPES

By Henry Dimbleby, Kay Plunkett-Hogge, Claire Ptak & John Vincent

PHOTOGRAPHY BY GEORGIA GLYNN SMITH · DESIGN BY ANITA MANGAN

conran
OCTOPUS

Contents

Introduction

Leon was founded on the belief that food should taste good and do you good.

You might think the recipes in this book only fulfill half that brief. They look indulgent, sound sinful, and taste like the sort of treats that normally come with a huge side order of guilt. Yet more than half these are wheat-free, sugar-free, or dairy-free recipes, with plenty of vegan and gluten-free options. This is a book that lets you have your cake and eat it.

It is also a little book. Secrete it in your briefcase for furtive commuter-time dreaming; take it to a friend's house for coffee; or on vacation so you can take a little bit of home baking with you. It is also the perfect size to slip into a loved one's Christmas stocking.

The recipes—selected from the best in the full-sized Leon cookbook—are designed to be straightforward, and there should be something here for any occasion. Taking the Better Brownie (see page 10) to work has been scientifically proven to make you more popular among your colleagues.

The Bar of Good Things (see page 26) is ideal for a guilt-free mid-morning snack or to put into a child's lunchbag. Try Violet's Coconut Macaroons (see page 39) for a refined afternoon tea party—it's one of those recipes that is impossibly easy, but creates something ridiculously sophisticated. Or, you could try baking a Spiced Honey & Orange Cake (see page 18) for something really voluptuous.

The Almond Date Oat Muffins (see page 48) are a perfect way to kickstart the day, or try our friend Rebecca's Salmon & Dill Muffins (see page 45) if you prefer your breakfast savory.

Most importantly, we want you to use this book. We hope it finds a permanent place in your kitchen and becomes batter-smattered, tacky with toffee, and dog-eared through use. Happy baking!

Henry & John

BROWNIES
& BARS

Better Brownie

MAKES 12 LARGE BROWNIES • PREPARATION TIME: 25 MINUTES • COOKING TIME: 25 MINUTES • ✓ WF GF

We have been selling these brownies at Leon since we opened our first restaurant in London's Carnaby Street in 2004. Made in Dorset by one of our favorite bakers, Emma Goss-Custard, the brownies are sugar and wheat free, but incredibly luxurious. Emma's stroke of genius was to add the little chunks of chocolate, providing the perfect contrast to the rich, gooey interior.

1½ sticks **unsalted butter**, plus extra for greasing
7 oz **semisweet chocolate** (54% cocoa solids)
1 **orange**
2 teaspoons **espresso** or **strong coffee**
½ cup **whole almonds** (skins on)
4 **eggs**

1 cup **ground almonds**
7 oz **semisweet chocolate** (54% cocoa solids), in chunks
7 oz **bittersweet chocolate** (70% cocoa solids), in chunks
¾ cup **fructose**
a pinch of **sea salt**
3–4 drops of **vanilla extract**

1. Heat the oven to 350°F. Generously butter a 12 x 8 x 2-inch baking pan, or one of similar dimensions.

2. Melt the butter in a small saucepan, and let it cool slightly.

3. In a separate bowl, melt the 7 oz of semisweet chocolate over a saucepan of hot water, stirring well to make sure that it is properly melted, and being careful not to burn it. Finely grate the orange zest directly into the melted chocolate to catch the oils that are released during the zesting process.

4. Add the coffee to the melted butter.

5. Spread out the almonds on a baking sheet and toast in the oven for 10 minutes, then coarsely chop.

6. Crack the eggs into a large mixing bowl. Add the ground almonds, the chopped almonds, all 14 oz of the chocolate chunks, and finally the fructose. Stir in the salt and vanilla, followed by the butter mixture and the melted semisweet chocolate.

7. Mix well until creamy and thickened, but do not overmix, because too much air will cause the brownie to crumble when baked.

8. Spoon the mixture into the prepared pan and bake for 20–25 minutes. Be careful not to overbake the brownies. They are ready when the edges are slightly crusty but the middle is still soft.

9. Remove from the oven. Let cool in the pan before slicing into 12 large brownies to serve.

TIPS

* Fructose turns a much darker color when baked than sugar. The brownie develops a glossy sheen and will not look cooked, when, in fact, it is. Resist the temptation to bake the brownies for too long.

* You can replace the fructose with 1 cup of sugar.

Flatplanet Brownies

MAKES 12–16 SLICES • PREPARATION TIME: 10 MINUTES PLUS COOLING
COOKING TIME: 1 HOUR 25 MINUTES • WF GF V

Although Leon is his first love, John has also spent some time on a little concept called Flatplanet. It's his attempt at creating a little café that recreates what was best about the original coffee shops, where people experience positivity, good food, and good ideas.

He's not the biggest fan of modern wheat. So at Flatplanet, they cook spelt flatbreads and wheat-free and gluten-free cakes, the most popular of which is this brownie.

Originally developed by Sarah Jenkins, these brownies are now made for Flatplanet by Sarah Hale and served with amazing energy in the store by Ot.

> 4 sticks **butter,** chopped
> 1 lb **chocolate** (minimum 50% cocoa solids), chopped
> 2 cups **superfine sugar**
> 6 **eggs**
> 3 cups **ground almonds**

1. Heat the oven to 250°F.

2. Over very low heat, melt the butter in a large saucepan. When almost melted, add the chocolate and stir until smooth. Remove the pan from the heat and stir in the sugar.

3. In a separate bowl, beat the eggs lightly together with a whisk. Then use the same whisk to beat them into the pan of chocolate mixture. Add the ground almonds, still mixing them in with the whisk until there are no large pockets of almonds remaining.

4. Grease and line a 10 x 14-inch baking pan. Pour the batter into the pan and bake in the oven for 1 hour 10 minutes, or until starting to crack on the surface.

5. Let the brownies cool in the pan for about an hour, because they will still be very soft.

6. When cool, slice, then remove from the pan and enjoy.

Tommi's More-Fruit-Than-Cake Cake

SERVES 8 • PREPARATION TIME: 25 MINUTES • COOKING TIME: 45 MINUTES • ✓ V

Red wine and figs have a special affinity for each other, and for the spices in this recipe. The fig seeds create a wonderful popping sensation as they burst in your mouth.

1⅔ cups **red wine**
1¾ cups **dried figs**, chopped
1½ teaspoons **ground cinnamon**
¼ teaspoon **ground cloves**
1 stick **unsalted butter**, cold
1 cup **honey**, plus extra for the top

1 **egg**, briefly beaten
1¾ cups **spelt flour**
1½ teaspoons **baking powder**
1 teaspoon **baking soda**

1. Heat the oven to 325°F. Line an 8 x 8-inch cake pan with parchment paper.

2. Put the red wine, figs, and spices into a medium saucepan over medium heat and bring to a boil.

3. When the fruit has plumped up a little (about 5 minutes), remove the saucepan from the heat and allow to cool for 10 minutes. Stir in the butter and honey and leave for another 10 minutes. Stir in the egg.

4. Sift the flour, baking power, and baking soda into a large mixing bowl. Pour the fig mixture onto the flour mixture and stir just until mixed. Pour into the prepared pan.

5. Bake for about 45 minutes, or until a toothpick inserted in the center comes out clean. Let cool in the pan. Drizzle the extra honey over the top to serve.

One of the great things about Claire is that her world is overflowing with cake. This cake got its name when she was at our house for dinner with our friend and fellow cook Tommi Miers. There wasn't any dessert, but Claire happened to have this experiment in her car outside. Tommi hasn't stopped talking about it since—"Best cake I have ever had. Just sitting there. In her car!"

HENRY

TIPS

* Serve with Greek yogurt or sour cream.

* A great way to use up leftover red wine. Can be served as a dessert or an afternoon snack. A chunk in your lunchbag also makes a delicious mid-morning snack.

Honey & Rose Baklava

MAKES 18–24 PIECES • PREPARATION TIME: 35 MINUTES PLUS COOLING • COOKING TIME: 1 HOUR • V

These are just one of the most beautiful things going—thin, crispy sheets of filigree-like pastry, delicate rose water, and fragrant honey.

12 sheets of **filo pastry** (have a few extra on standby if you're clumsy)
1¾ sticks **unsalted butter**, melted
an extra tablespoon of **orange blossom honey**, to finish (optional)

For the syrup:
⅓ cup **orange blossom honey**
¼ cup **water**
¼ cup **superfine sugar**
2 tablespoons **rose water**
a pinch of **ground cinnamon**
2 **star anise**

For the filling:
1 cup firmly packed **soft brown sugar**
1 cup shelled **pistachios**
1 cup **walnut pieces**
1 cup **ground almonds**
¼ cup **flaxseeds**, toasted
1 teaspoon **ground cinnamon**
the seeds from 10 **cardamom pods**
1 tablespoon **dried rose petals** (optional)

1. Heat the oven to 350°F. Grease a 12 x 8½-inch baking pan.

2. Put all the filling ingredients into a food processor and process until broken down. You want some texture so don't grind it to a paste. Tip the mixture into a bowl and set aside.

3. Unroll the filo pastry and cut the sheets in half—they should be about 12 x 8½ inches when cut. (Keep the sheets covered with a damp dish towel, because they dry out.)

4. Layer the pastry sheets in the baking pan, one at a time, brushing each sheet with melted butter until you have stacked 10 sheets. Spoon an even layer of filling on top of the tenth sheet. Then place another sheet on top and butter again. Add another layer of filling and repeat the layers until the filling is used up—it will probably take 2 more layers. Finish with 10 sheets of filo layered on top, remembering to butter every sheet as you work, then butter the top sheet on top.

5. Cut the baklava diagonally into diamond shapes.

6. Place in the oven for 45 minutes to 1 hour. (Check them after 45 minutes: you want a golden-brown crisp exterior.)

7. Meanwhile, make the syrup. Gently heat the syrup ingredients in a saucepan over medium heat and simmer for 5–10 minutes, or until thick and fragrant. Remove from the heat and let cool.

8. As soon as the baklava comes out of the oven, pour the cooled syrup evenly over the surface. Finish by drizzling the extra tablespoon of honey on the top, if you want to, and sprinkle it with any leftover filling. Let the baklava cool in the pan before gently transferring it to a serving plate. If you're feeling fancy, decorate the cooled baklava with a scattering of dried rose petals.

Spiced Honey & Orange Cake

MAKES 18-24 PIECES • PREPARATION TIME: 15 MINUTES • COOKING TIME: 2 HOURS • GF V

Kay's husband Fred is obsessed with those gooey, sticky-but-oh-so-good honey cakes sold in Middle Eastern bakeries. From his travels in Lebanon and Syria, this one has the taste he remembers, but without the flour. It's a moist, dense cake, drenched in honey and orange flower syrup and is best served with mint tea or strong coffee.

1 **orange**
3 **eggs**
1 cup **superfine sugar**
1 tablespoon **orange blossom honey**
1½ cups **ground almonds**
½ cup **walnuts, ground**
2 tablespoons **buckwheat flour**
1 teaspoon **gluten-free baking powder**
¼ teaspoon **ground cinnamon**
¼ teaspoon **ground ginger**
the seeds from 8–10 **cardamom pods**, lightly crushed
a pinch of **salt**

For the syrup:
¼ cup **orange blossom honey**
2 tablespoons **orange flower water**

1. Put the orange into a large saucepan of boiling water. Bring back to a boil and simmer for 50–60 minutes, or until tender. Drain and set aside to cool slightly. Cut the orange into quarters, remove any seeds, and place in a food processor. Blend until smooth.

2. Heat the oven to 350°F. Grease a 9 x 9-inch cake pan and line with wax paper or parchment paper.

3. Add the eggs and sugar to a bowl and beat together. Then add the tablespoon of honey and beat again. Stir in the ground almonds and walnuts, the buckwheat flour, and the spices. Add the pureed orange and stir well to combine.

4. Scrape the batter into the prepared pan. Bake for 50–60 minutes, or until a little springy and deep golden brown. Let it cool in its pan.

5. To make the syrup, heat the honey and orange flower water in a saucepan over gentle heat and stir until combined.

6. When the cake has completely cooled, lift it out of the pan but keep it on its paper. Drizzle the top with syrup using a spoon. Let the cake absorb the syrup then cut into small squares to serve.

Sally Dolton's Granola Bars

MAKES 16 • PREPARATION TIME: 15 MINUTES • COOKING TIME: 20 MINUTES • ♥ ✓ DF V

Sally is a Leon regular who sent us this recipe for her granola bars when we mentioned that we were writing a second cookbook. They are really, really good.

1½ cups **dried fruit** (e.g. apricots, figs, dates
  pears, etc.: use a mixture or choose just one)
½ cup **nuts** (e.g. cashew nuts)
½ cup **seed**s (e.g. pumpkin seeds,
  sunflower seeds)
1 teaspoon **ground cinnamon**
⅓ cup **fruit juic**e (e.g. apple or grape)
2 level tablespoons **honey**
½ cup **whole-wheat flour**
1⅓ cups **rolled oats**

1. Preheat the oven to 375°F.

2. Put the dried fruit into a food processor and process until well chopped. Do the same with the nuts. Add the fruit, nuts, seeds, and cinnamon to a bowl.

3. Heat together the fruit juice and honey in a saucepan large enough to eventually hold all the ingredients. When the honey has dissolved add the flour and oats, and then stir in the fruit and nuts.

4. Smooth the mixture into a 10 x 12-inch baking pan about 1 inch deep. If the baking pan is not nonstick line it with parchment paper before use.

5. Bake in the oven for 20 minutes—longer if you would like your bars more crunchy.

6. Let cool, then cut into rectangular bars. They will keep for 2 weeks in an airtight container.

TIPS

* Try adding a handful of grated fresh ginger.

Nana Goy's Cranberry Oat Bars

MAKES 16 • PREPARATION TIME: 10 MINUTES • COOKING TIME: 30–35 MINUTES • V

These are moist and deliciously oaty, just the way a good oat bar should be. We love them with dried cranberries but you could use any dried fruits (see tips below).

1½ cups **dried cranberries**
¼ cup **light corn syrup**
1½ sticks **butter**
½ cup **superfine sugar**
2¾ cups **rolled oats**

1. Heat the oven to 340°F, and butter an 8 x 8-inch baking pan.

2. Put the cranberries into a bowl and cover with boiling water for a few minutes to rehydrate them. Drain away the water and roughly chop any that are particularly large.

3. Melt together the syrup, butter, and sugar in a large saucepan over low heat until the sugar has dissolved, then stir in the oats. Add all but a small handful of the cranberries and stir thoroughly.

4. Tip the oat mixture into the baking pan and smooth it down with a spatula. Sprinkle the remaining cranberries on top. Bake in the oven for 30–35 minutes, or until golden. Mark into squares while still warm, and remove from the pan once cool.

TIPS

* Add a handful of nuts and seeds to the mixture if you want to bring another dimension to these oat bars.

* For a fruity hit, try making them with dates instead of cranberries. If you choose to do this, chop the dates roughly before adding to the oat mixture.

Elisabeth's Lemon Bars

MAKES 8–10 • PREPARATION TIME: 30 MINUTES • COOKING TIME: I HOUR •

Sweet and gooey, with a sharp finish. An indulgent treat.

2¼ cups **all-purpose flour**,
   plus an extra ¼ cup
⅔ cup **confectioners' sugar**,
   plus extra for dusting
1 teaspoon **salt**
2 sticks **cold unsalted butter**

4 **eggs**
1¾ cups **superfine sugar**
½ cup **fresh lemon juice**
½ teaspoon grated **lemon zest**
1 teaspoon **baking powder**

1. Heat the oven to 340°F.

2. First make the shortbread crust. Combine the 2¼ cups flour, confectioners' sugar, salt, and cold butter in a food processor and mix until crumbly. If you don't have a food processor, cut the butter up with two knives (I always find this tricky), the back of a fork, or an old-fashioned pastry cutter (I prefer the latter).

3. Be careful not to let the butter get too warm in either the appliance or your hands, because it changes the texture. Mix until the dough just forms a ball.

4. Press the dough evenly into the bottom of a 12 x 8-inch baking pan.

5. Bake in the oven for 20–25 minutes, or until golden and set, then let cool slightly while you make with the topping.

6. Beat the eggs in a bowl. Add the sugar, lemon juice, and lemon zest. In a separate bowl, sift together the remaining ¼ cup flour and the baking powder. Add to the egg mixture and stir to combine. Spread onto the cooled shortbread crust and return to the oven for 25–30 minutes, or until just set.

7. Let cool completely in the pan. Dust generously with confectioners' sugar and cut into squares or diamonds. These will keep well in an airtight container for up to 3 days.

TIPS

* Scatter with lavender flowers if you have them growing in your yard.

Bar of Good Things

MAKES 8 BARS · PREPARATION TIME: 20 MINUTES PLUS SOAKING TIME FOR SEEDS
COOKING TIME: 2 HOURS · ♥ ✓ WF GF DF V

This recipe makes a healthy bar, and will keep you going on a long hike or make a great recharger after exercising.

1 cup **sesame seeds**, preferably soaked and dried
1 cup **cashew nuts**, finely chopped
a pinch of **sea salt**
2 tablespoons **brown rice syrup**
2 tablespoons **tahini**
2 tablespoons **yacon syrup**
2 teaspoons **lemon zest**
1½ cups **salted pistachios,** shelled and coarsely chopped
⅔ cup **dried apricots**, chopped

For the fig paste
¼ cup **water**
1 teaspoon **vanilla extract**
1 cup **dried figs**
1¼ teaspoons **ground ginger**
¼ teaspoon **ground cumin**

For the coating
½ cup **sesame seeds**, lightly toasted

1. Heat the oven to 225°F. Line a 12 x 8-inch baking pan with parchment paper. Heat the water with the vanilla in a small saucepan and pour it onto the dried figs. Allow to rest for 15 minutes, then blend with the ginger and cumin to form a paste.

2. Meanwhile, mix the sesame seeds, cashew nuts, and salt in a medium bowl. Mix the brown rice syrup, tahini, yacon, and lemon zest in a small bowl and stir in the fig paste.

3. Add the wet ingredients to the dry ingredients and mix well. This is easiest done with your hands, because the mixture should be stiff. Then fold in the pistachios and apricots.

4. Sprinkle half the sesame seeds for the coating into the prepared pan and then press the mixture evenly on top so it is about ½ inch in thickness. Sprinkle with the remaining seeds.

5. Bake in the oven for 1 hour, then flip it over and bake for another hour. Cool in the pan, cut into bars, and store in an airtight container.

TIPS

* The yacon syrup can be replaced by more brown rice syrup or agave syrup.

George's Ice Cream Sandwich

MAKE: 12 DISKS • PREPARATION TIME: 20 MINUTES + 2 HOURS SOAKING
COOKING TIME: 2 HOURS • ♥ ✓ WF GF DF V

An indulgent treat for you and any children in your life.

1⅓ cup **almonds**
⅓ cup shelled **hemp seeds**
¾ cup chopped **fresh dates**
seeds of ½ **vanilla bean**
a pinch of **sea salt**
ice cream, for the filling

1. Soak the almonds in water for 2 hours, drain, then crush to a paste using a mortar and pestle or a food processor.

2. Heat the oven to 225°F.

3. Add the hemp seeds, chopped dates, vanilla seeds, and salt to the almonds and bring everything together by pounding or processing for a few seconds.

4. Press out onto parchment paper and roll to ⅛ inch thickness. Use round cookie cutters to cut 2-inch circles. Reroll any excess to get 12 circles. Place in the oven to dry out for 2 hours.

5. To make the ice cream sandwich: take a scoop of your favorite ice cream and sandwich it between 2 circles. Hand to small child. Be prepared to load washing machine. (Don't worry, it doesn't stain.)

I like these chewy cookies so much for their texture and lovely flavor. One of the wonderful benefits of eating sweets and cakes that are made with alternative ingredients is that they usually satisfy your cravings much better and, therefore, you eat less of them.

CLAIRE

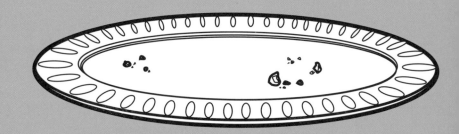

COOKIES

Cut-out Cookies

MAKES 24 (DEPENDING ON SIZE) • PREPARATION TIME: 15 MINUTES PLUS 2 HOURS CHILLING
COOKING TIME: 15 MINUTES • V

You need the right kind of dough to make cut-out cookies—one that holds its shape during baking. This recipe should be a cornerstone of your baking repertoire, especially if you have young children. Make these crumbly, light cookies for Christmas, children's parties, or just because it's a great way to keep the kids entertained.

2 sticks **unsalted butter**, very soft
2 cups **superfine sugar**
2 **eggs**
1 teaspoon **vanilla extract**

4½ cups **all-purpose flour**
1 teaspoon **baking powder**
a pinch of **salt**
ready-to-use icing, to decorate

1. With an electric handheld mixer, beat the softened butter with the superfine sugar until light, pale, and fluffy.

2. Add the eggs, one by one, then the vanilla extract.

3. Weigh the flour into a separate bowl and whisk in the baking powder and salt. Add half of this to the creamed mixture and beat on low speed until just combined.

4. Add the remaining flour mixture and beat again to combine well.

5. Divide the dough in half and seal each ball in plastic wrap. Chill for about 2 hours or overnight before using. You could freeze one ball to use another time, if you like.

6. When you are ready to make the cookies, heat the oven to 325°F. Line a couple of cookie sheets with parchment paper.

7. Lightly dust a work surface with flour, then roll out the dough to about ¼ inch thick. Cut out shapes with your cookie cutters and transfer the cookies to your prepared cookie sheets. Chill for 15–20 minutes, then bake for 15 minutes, or until just starting to turn golden. Transfer to a wire rack and leave to cool completely.

8. Decorate the cookies with icing and let stand overnight to dry.

9. Store in an airtight container for up to a week.

Maggie's Best Chocolate Chip Cookies

MAKES 24 • PREPARATION TIME: 15 MINUTES • COOKING TIME: 11 MINUTES • WF GF V

Gooey, chocolatey, but without the flour or sugar.

2¼ cups **gluten-free flour**
2 teaspoons **baking soda**
½ teaspoon **sea salt**
1 cup **semisweet chocolate chips** or chunks
3 tablespoons **agave syrup**

1 cup **maple syrup**
1 stick **unsalted butter**, melted
1 tablespoon **vanilla extract**
sea salt, for sprinkling (optional)

1. Heat the oven to 350°F. Line a cookie sheet with parchment paper.

2. Mix together all the dry ingredients in a medium bowl (including the chocolate chips or chunks).

3. Mix together all the wet ingredients in a small bowl.

4. Add the wet ingredients to the dry ingredients, and stir until they are well combined, but do not overmix.

5. Drop spoonfuls of the cookie dough onto the prepared cookie sheet spaced slightly apart. Lightly sprinkle with sea salt if desired.

6. Bake in the oven for only 11 minutes, then let them cool on the cookie sheet for 1 minute before transferring them to a wire rack.

Once you have got the hang of these, you can play around with the recipe. We like to substitute white chocolate and dried blueberries for the semisweet chocolate, and add milk chocolate and toasted pecans, or walnuts or hazelnuts in with the semisweet chocolate in the original recipe. Maggie is one of the bakers we love. In her original recipe, she uses all-purpose flour, not gluten free, and maple sugar instead of agave syrup. She also sometimes adds a ½ teaspoon of molasses, which sounds divine.

CLAIRE

TIPS

*   These are even better the next day. Enjoy with a glass of cold hazelnut milk.

*   Following the baking time recommended here will give you the perfect gooey texture.

*   If you can't get hold of gluten-free flour and you don't mind the gluten, normal flour can be substituted.

Lise's Cherry Almond Cookies

WITH CHOCOLATE CHIPS

MAKES 15–20 • PREPARATION TIME: 20 MINUTES • COOKING TIME: 10–12 MINUTES • V

The recipe below is based on Lise's oat and raisin cookie, which we serve in the restaurant, but with a sweet summer twist. If you want to make a version of the original, just replace the chocolate chips, cherries, and almonds with raisins (see picture).

1¾ sticks **salted butter**, softened
1 cup firmly packed **brown sugar**
2 small **eggs**
1 cup **all-purpose flour**
½ teaspoon **baking soda**

2 cups **rolled oats**
1 cup **dried sour cherries**
½ cup **slivered almonds**
½ cup **chocolate chips**

1. Heat the oven to 350°F. Oil several large cookie sheets or line them with parchment paper.

2. Cream together the butter and the sugar, then add the eggs, one at a time, and beat until light and fluffy.

3. In another bowl, combine the flour, baking soda, oats, cherries, sllivered almonds, and chocolate chips. Add to the butter mixture, being careful not to overmix the dough.

4. Scoop the dough into balls about 2 inches in diameter, using an ice cream scoop. (You can also use 2 tablespoons.) Place the dough balls on the prepared cookie sheets 10 inches apart. Each cookie will spread to about 4 inches. If your dough is cold, the cookies will not spread as well, in which case you will need to press them with the palm of your hand before baking.

5. Bake in the oven for 10–12 minutes, or until golden (you may need to bake them in batches). The cookies will be very soft when you take them out, but will become firmer as they cool down. Let them cool on the cookie sheets for a few minutes before transferring them to a wire rack to cool completely. Store in an airtight container.

Lise learned to love baking in her mother's kitchen. Her mother had a fruit and vegetable garden outside her kitchen in the Danish countryside, next to the wild pine forests that sloped gently down to the sea. Everything was organic in her mother's kitchen, and still is now, in Lise's Honeyrose Bakery.

VIOLET Coconut Macaroons

MAKES 12 • PREPARATION TIME: 5 MINUTES • COOKING TIME: 15 MINUTES • ♥ WF GF DF

There is a sublime crispy gooiness to these macaroons that makes them like nothing else on earth. Warning: they are very addictive. Violet is the name of Claire's bakery and shop on Wilton Way and her stand at Broadway Market, both in Hackney, London.

3 **egg whites**
¾ cup **superfine sugar**
a pinch of **salt**
2 teaspoons of **honey**
2 cups **dry, unsweetened shredded coconut**
½ teaspoon **vanilla extract**

1. Heat the oven to 300°F. Line a cookie sheet with parchment paper.

2. Combine the egg whites, sugar, salt, honey, and coconut in a large pan over medium heat.

3. Stir the mixture constantly until everything is dissolved and it just begins to scorch on the bottom.

4. Take the pan off the heat and stir in the vanilla extract.

5. Let the mixture cool completely, then use an ice cream scoop (about ¼ cup capacity) to scoop out 12 even macaroons, and place them on the prepard cookie sheet.

6. Bake in the oven for about 10–15 minutes, or until golden and set. Let the macaroons cool completely before peeling off the paper.

TIPS

* The key to getting these macaroons just right is to stir the ingredients in the pan until they begin to dry out.

* The vanilla extract isn't essential.

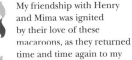

My friendship with Henry and Mima was ignited by their love of these macaroons, as they returned time and time again to my market stand to buy them.

CLAIRE

Oat Crackers

MAKES 12 • PREPARATION TIME: 15 MINUTES PLUS 30 MINUTES CHILLING
COOKING TIME: 10 MINUTES • ✓ V

These savory crackers are buttery and crumbly and the best thing to eat with a hard cheese. Also wonderful spread with a nut butter.

2¾ cups rolled **oats**
1⅓ cups **spelt flour**, plus extra
    for dusting
1 cup **whole-wheat spelt flour**

½ teaspoon **baking soda**
2¼ sticks **unsalted butter**
1 teaspoon **salt**
1 **egg**

1. Mix together the oats, spelt flours, and baking soda. Rub the butter into the oatmeal mixture between your fingertips until it just about disappears.

2. Add the salt and egg to bring the dough together, then chill for at least 30 minutes.

3. Meanwhile heat the oven to 350°F and line a cookie sheet with parchment paper.

4. Roll out the dough to about ⅛ inch thickness on a lightly floured work surface. Cut out the crackers with a round cookie cutter, or cut a circle of dough 7 inches in diameter and then cut that into 4 wedges.

5. Place the crackers on the cookie sheet and bake for 8–10 minutes. They will crisp up as they cool. They should be eaten fresh or kept in an airtight container for up to a week.

TIPS

* These crackers will absorb moisture and become soft if left out, but they can be recrisped (as can any crackers containing butter) by laying them out on a cookie sheet lined with parchment paper and placing them into a preheated oven at 325°F for 5 minutes.

* A Christmas essential with Stilton cheese.

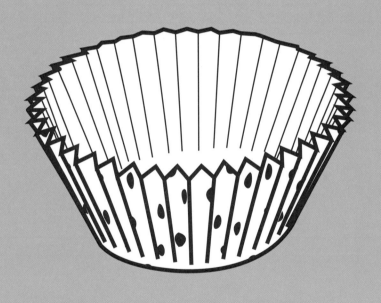

MUFFINS CUPCAKES & BUNS

Salmon & Dill Muffins

MAKES 6 · PREPARATION TIME: 15 MINUTES · COOKING TIME: 20 MINUTES

A savory breakfast muffin.

2 cups **all-purpose flour**
2 teaspoons **baking powder**
1½ cups **grated cheese**
2 oz chopped **smoked salmon**
⅓ cup chopped **fresh dill**
1 **egg**
¾ cup **buttermilk**
⅓ cup **vegetable** or **sunflower oil**
½ cup **cream cheese**

1. Heat the oven to 350°F, and line a 6-hole muffin pan with paper baking cups.

2. Mix the flour and baking powder together in a large bowl. Add the grated cheese, smoked salmon, and dill.

3. In a separate bowl beat together the egg, buttermilk, and oil.

4. Place half the wet ingredients into the dry ingredients and stir well. Then add the rest of the wet ingredients and mix just until combined.

5. Spoon into the paper baking cups until each is half full, then place a heaping teaspoon of cream cheese in the middle of each muffin. Add more batter until each baking cup is full.

6. Bake for 10 minutes, then remove the pan from the oven and turn it around so the muffins cook evenly. Put the pan back into the oven and continue to bake for a further 10 minutes, or until the muffins are just browning on top.

Our friend Rebecca used to make these for us painstakingly every day at home and then drive them to the restaurants daily. Sadly (for us) she is now the proud mother of two and the muffins are no longer to be found in Leon. If you liked them, here they are.

HENRY

45

George Pickard's Cheese & Ham Muffins

A great snack instead of sugary cookies for when children get home from school.

6 slices of **ham**
1⅔ cups **Cheddar cheese**
⅓ cup **butter**
1 **egg**
1 cup **milk**
2⅓ cups **all-purpose flour**
3½ teaspoons **baking powder**
½ teaspoon **paprika**
a pinch of **sea salt**

1. Preheat the oven to 375°F. Lightly grease a 12-hole muffin pan.

2. Cut the ham into ½-inch chunks, and shred the Cheddar cheese or chop it coarsely. Cut the butter into pieces. Beat the egg in a bowl with the milk.

3. Sift the flour, baking powder, paprika, and salt into a large bowl, and rub the butter into the flour until it looks like bread crumbs.

4. Add the ham and cheese, then pour in the egg and milk mixture and mix thoroughly.

5. Spoon the batter into the muffin pan, place in the oven, and bake for 20 minutes.

6. Place on a wire rack to cool.

George loves cooking and learned this recipe at school. I often find him in the kitchen making these on his own. Sadly they don't last very long, because they are delicious!

APPLE

Almond Date Oat Muffins

MAKES 12 • PREPARATION TIME: 20 MINUTES • COOKING TIME: 25 MINUTES • ✓ ♥ V

A nutty, semisweet breakfast muffin made with spelt flour, which is not only better for you than other varieties of wheat, but gives a distinctive texture and flavor.

¾ cup **whole almonds**, skins on
1¾ sticks **unsalted butter**, melted
⅓ cup **light brown sugar**
2 cups **oat bran**
1 cup **rolled oats**, plus extra
   for sprinkling on the muffins
1¾ cups **fine spelt flour**

½ teaspoon **salt**
1½ teaspoons **baking soda**
2 **eggs**
1½ cups **plain yogurt**
2 cups **pitted chopped dates**
zest from 1 **orange**

1. Heat the oven to 340°F. Butter a muffin pan or line it with paper baking cups.

2. Spread out the almonds on a baking sheet and toast in the oven for 5–7 minutes, or until golden.

3. Melt the butter and sugar in a small saucepan and set aside to cool slightly.

4. In a large bowl, mix together the oat bran, rolled oats, spelt flour, salt, and baking soda. Coarsely chop the toasted almonds and stir them into the dry ingredients.

5. In a new bowl, whisk together the eggs and yogurt and stir in the dates and orange zest. Whisk in the melted butter and sugar and pour all of this onto the dry ingredients. Mix just until combined.

6. Spoon the batter into the muffin pan and bake in the oven for 20–25 minutes.

TIPS

* You could also make these muffins with dates that have been soaked in juice or alcohol.

This muffin is inspired by one I learned to make at the wonderful Bovine Bakery, in Point Reyes, California. I started my career there, aged fifteen, under the tutelage of Deborah Ruff and Bridget Devlin. I learned so much from them, not only about baking, but about running a small business. This muffin is my homage to them.

CLAIRE

Sugar-free Vanilla Cupcakes

MAKES: 12 • PREPARATION TIME: 15 MINUTES • COOKING TIME: 25 MINUTES • ♥ ✓ WF GF DF V

A cupcake free of everything except indulgence. No one will ever believe they are so good for you.

2¼ cups **gluten-free flour**
3¼ teaspoons **gluten-free baking powder**
⅔ cup **potato flour**
  (or ¾ cup **cornstarch**)
1 cup **coconut flour** (fine dry coconut)
1 tablespoon **flaxseed meal** (optional)

1½ teaspoons **sea salt**
⅔ cup **coconut oil**, melted
1 cup **agave syrup**
2 tablespoons **vanilla extract**
⅔ cup **rice milk**
½ teaspoon **baking soda**
½ cup **boiling water**

1. Heat the oven to 340°F, and line a 12-hole muffin pan with paper baking cups.

2. Sift the gluten-free flour, potato flour (or cornstarch), coconut flour, flaxseed meal (if using), and sea salt into a large bowl, or use a whisk to mix them together.

3. In another bowl, combine the melted coconut oil, agave syrup, vanilla extract, and rice milk. In a small bowl, mix together the baking soda and boiling water and then stir this into the other liquid ingredients.

4. Pour one-third of the liquid ingredients into the dry and beat together to make a batter, gradually adding the remaining liquid until all of it is incorporated.

5. Spoon the batter into the paper baking cups and bake in the oven for 20–25 minutes, or until a skewer inserted in the center of a cupcake comes out clean. These are best eaten on the day they are made.

TIPS

* The flaxseed meal can be left out if you can't find it at your local health food store, but it adds nutrition and a nutty quality that we like, and also adds texture.

* If you don't like the flavor of coconut (you're crazy), you can replace the coconut flour with ground almonds, and the coconut oil with a good-quality tasteless oil, such as sunflower, but only if you *really* must. Coconut oil is full of nutrients.

Vegan Vanilla Frosting

MAKES ENOUGH TO FROST 12 CUPCAKES • PREPARATION TIME: 15 MINUTES PLUS COOLING
COOKING TIME: NONE • ♥ ✓ WF GF DF V

We think this frosting might be even better than the traditional buttercream version.
It is the result of weeks spent by Claire testing different dairy- and allergen-free
combinations. It is rich, but the coconut oil gives it a sublime melting consitency.

1½ cups **unsweetened soy milk**,
1 cup **very finely ground almonds**
¼ cup **agave syrup**
2 teaspoons **vanilla extract**
1 **vanilla bean**, seeds scraped out

1½ cups **coconut oil**, melted
2 tablespoons **fresh orange**
   or **clementine juice**
1 tablespoon **fresh lemon juice**
¼ cup **cashew nut butter**

1. With an immersion blender or in a food processor, combine the soy
   milk, finely ground almonds, agave, and vanilla. Blend until smooth.

2. Add the scraped seeds from the vanilla bean and keep the bean for
   another use.

3. Combine the melted coconut oil with the orange and lemon juice
   and add to the mixture gradually, blending until smooth. Add the
   cashew nut butter and again blend until smooth.

4. Chill overnight before using so that the
   coconut oil solidifies.

TIPS

* For pink frosting replace ⅔ cup of
  the soy milk with ⅔ cup of pureed,
  strained raspberries or strawberries.

* You can play with other natural
  colors and flavors.

* If you can't do soy, substitute rice
  milk for the soy milk. The texture
  is not quite as smooth but the
  taste is great.

Zucchini Mini Cupcakes

MAKES 12 • PREPARATION TIME: 20 MINUTES PLUS COOLING • COOKING TIME: 30 MINUTES • ✓ GF V

There is a small deli in John's nearest village and the thing John likes most about it is the gluten-free zucchini mini cupcakes. This is our version of the little beauties.

1 stick **butter, softened**
½ cup firmly packed **light brown sugar**
2 **egg**
1⅓ cup **gluten-free flour**
2 teaspoons **baking powder**
1 teaspoon **ground cinnamon**
½ teaspoon **ground allspice**
juice and zest of 1 **orange** or 1 **lemon**
1½ cups shredded **zucchini**
¼ cup coarsely chopped **walnuts** (optional)

For the lemon or orange cream cheese frosting:
2 tablespoons **unsalted butter,** softened
¼ cup **cream cheese**
1¼ cups **confectioners' sugar**
the juice and zest of ¼ of a **lemon** or **orange**

TIPS

* Why not make these with less sugar and have them for breakfast?

1. Heat the oven to 350°F. Line a 12-hole mini cupcake pan with paper baking cups.

2. Beat the butter and sugar together in a mixing bowl until creamy. Add an egg and stir it in. Do the same with the second egg.

3. Sift the flour, baking powder, cinnamon, and ground allspice into a bowl. Fold the flour mixture into the butter, sugar, and eggs, stopping halfway through to add the orange or lemon juice and zest. Then stir in the zucchini, and walnuts (if using).

4. Scoop a large tablespoonful of the mixture into each baking cup then set the mini cupcake pan onto a cookie sheet. Set this into the oven and bake for 30 minutes.

5. Remove from the oven and set the cupcake pan on a rack to cool.

6. To make the frosting, beat the butter and cream cheese together, and gradually add the confectioners' sugar and the lemon or orange juice and zest. Frost the mini cupcakes once they have cooled down.

Jossy's Casablanca Cakes

Perfect with ice cream.

⅓ cup **almonds**, with skins
zest of 1 **lemon**
1 **large egg**
¾ cup **confectioners' sugar**, plus extra for dipping
½ teaspoon **baking powder**
½ cup **semolina**

1. Preheat the oven to 325°F.

2. Put the almonds into a food processor and grind as finely as possible. Grate the zest from the lemon and reserve.

3. Whisk the egg with the confectioners' sugar until very pale. Stir in the baking powder, semolina, ground almonds, and lemon zest. Mix thoroughly to combine.

4. Butter a large cookie sheet and sift some confectioners' sugar into a small bowl. Dampen your hands, take a piece of the dough, and form a ball the size of a large marble. Dip one side of the ball into the confectioners' sugar and place it on the cookie sheet, sugar-side up.

5. Continue like this with the rest of the mixture, spacing the balls 2 inches apart—they spread a lot during baking. You will probably have to bake them in two batches.

6. Bake the cakes in the center of the oven for 10–12 minutes, or until very pale brown. Ease carefully off the baking sheet with a spatula and cool on a rack.

These were inspired by a trip to Morocco many years ago when Henry was a young child; he and his sisters loved these quickly made half-cookies, half-cakes.

JOSSY

Spelt Hot Cross Buns

MAKES 12 • PREPARATION TIME: 50 MINUTES + 3½–3¾ HOURS RISING TIME
COOKING TIME: 15 MINUTES • ♥ ✓ DF V

Wholesome and delicious. These buns are a little less sweet than most hot cross buns but just as festive. Toast them and slather with butter—or coconut oil if you don't do dairy. You can make the dough the day before, put them into the fridge overnight, and bake them fresh in the morning on Easter Day.

2 x 14-oz envelopes of **dry active yeast**
1 cup **rice milk**, warmed slightly, plus extra to brush the tops
1 cup **agave syrup**
2¼ cups **strong whole-wheat spelt flour**
2¼ cups **all-purpose spelt flour**
1 teaspoon **salt**
½ teaspoon **ground allspice**
½ teaspoon freshly grated **nutmeg**
1 teaspoon **ground cinnamon**

½ cup **currants**
½ cup **golden raisins**
zest of 1 **orange**
1 **egg** or **egg substitute**
¼ cup **coconut oil**, melted

For the crosses:
⅔ cup **all-purpose spelt flour**
1 tablespoon **water**

For the bun wash:
⅓ cup **water**
½ cup **agave syrup**

1. Preheat the oven to 425°F. Line 2 baking sheets with parchment paper.

2. Dissolve the yeast in the warm rice milk with the agave and set aside.

3. In a separate bowl, combine the flours, salt, spices, currants, golden raisins, and orange zest.

4. Add the egg or egg substitute and the coconut oil to the milk mixture, then pour all of this onto the dry ingredients. Stir to combine. When it comes together as dough let it rest for about 20 minutes.

5. Turn the dough out onto a floured surface and knead it for 10–12 minutes, or until it becomes silky. Put it back into the bowl and cover with a clean cloth. Leave in a warm place until the dough has nearly doubled in bulk. This should take about 3 hours.

6. Divide the dough into 12 pieces. Roll each piece into a ball and place on the prepared baking sheets, about 1 inch apart. Leave them to rise for about 30–45 minutes, while you prepare the crosses.

7. When the buns have risen, brush them with a little rice milk. Put the ⅔ cup of flour for the crosses into a small bowl and stir in about 1 tablespoon of water to make a paste. Use a pastry bag with a small round tip (or make one out of parchment paper) to pipe the paste in crosses on each bun. Bake in the oven for about 15 minutes, or until golden brown.

8. While the rolls are baking, make the "bun wash" by gently heating the water and agave syrup in a small saucepan.

9. As soon as the buns come out of the oven, brush them with the bun wash. Serve warm or toasted, with your favorite spreads.

Good Scones

MAKES 12 • PREPARATION TIME: 25 MINUTES • COOKING TIME: 25 MINUTES • ♥ ✓ DF V

These scones are made with plenty of alternative ingredients that make them healthier. But we like the idea of eating them with clotted cream anyway.

¾ cup **gluten-free all-purpose flour**
1 cup **white spelt flour**
2 teaspoons **gluten-free baking powder**
a large pinch of **salt**
¼ cup **coconut oil**, melted, or **sunflower oil**
2 tablespoons **maple syrup**
1 tablespoon **vanilla extract**
⅓ cup **hot water**
3 tablespoons **rice milk**
clotted cream or **cream substitute** and
    fresh **strawberry jam**, to serve

1. Measure all the dry ingredients into a large bowl and stir to combine. In a small saucepan, melt the coconut oil and let it cool slightly. Pour the oil onto the dry ingredients and toss together with a fork.

2. Mix the remaining ingredients, except the cream and jam, into the dry ingredients until just combined to a dough. Don't overwork it.

3. Let the dough rest for 10 minutes. Meanwhile line a baking sheet with parchment paper, and heat the oven to 350°F.

4. Roll out the dough ½–¾ inch thick. Use a round cookie cutter or a drinking glass to cut out disks.

5. Place the scones on the baking sheet and bake for 20–25 minutes.

6. When they are ready and firm to the touch, take them out of the oven and place on a cooling rack. Cool completely before splitting open and filling with cream and jam.

TIPS

* You could make the scones wheat free by omitting the spelt flour and using either more of the gluten-free flour or substituting gram flour for the spelt.

CONVERSION CHART FOR COMMON MEASURES

LIQUIDS

15 ml	$^1/_2$ fl oz
25 ml	1 fl oz
50 ml	2 fl oz
75 ml	3 fl oz
100ml	3 $^1/_2$ fl oz
125 ml	4 fl oz
150 ml	$^1/_4$ pint
175 ml	6 fl oz
200 ml	7 fl oz
250 ml	8 fl oz
275 ml	9 fl oz
300 ml	$^1/_2$ pint
325 ml	11 fl oz
350 ml	12 fl oz
375 ml	13 fl oz
400 ml	14 fl oz
450 ml	$^3/_4$ pint
475 ml	16 fl oz
500 ml	17 fl oz
575 ml	18 fl oz
600 ml	1 pint
750 ml	1 $^1/_4$ pints
900 ml	1 $^1/_2$ pints
1 liter	1 $^3/_4$ pints
1.2 liters	2 pints
1.5 liters	2 $^1/_2$ pints
1.8 liters	3 pints
2 liters	3 $^1/_2$ pints
2.5 liters	4 pints
3.6 liters	6 pints

WEIGHTS

5 g	$^1/_4$ oz
15 g	$^1/_2$ oz
20 g	$^3/_4$ oz
25 g	1 oz
50 g	2 oz
75 g	3 oz
125 g	4 oz
150 g	5 oz
175 g	6 oz
200 g	7 oz
250 g	8 oz
275 g	9 oz
300 g	10 oz
325 g	11 oz
375 g	12 oz
400 g	13 oz
425 g	14 oz
475 g	15 oz
500 g	1 lb
625 g	1 $^1/_4$ lb
750 g	1 $^1/_2$ lb
875 g	1 $^3/_4$ lb
1 kg	2 lb
1.25 kg	2 $^1/_2$ lb
1.5 kg	3 lb
1.75 kg	3 $^1/_2$ lb
2 kg	4 lb

OVEN TEMPERATURES

225°F........(110°C) .....Gas Mark $^1/_4$
250°F ......(120°C) ......Gas Mark $^1/_2$
275°F ......(140°C) ......Gas Mark 1
300°F ......(150°C) ......Gas Mark 2
325°F ......(160°C) ......Gas Mark 3
350°F ......(180°C) ......Gas Mark 4
375°F ......(190°C) ......Gas Mark 5
400°F ......(200°C) ......Gas Mark 6
425°F ......(220°C) ......Gas Mark 7
450°F ......(230°C) ......Gas Mark 8

MEASUREMENTS

5 mm .... $^1/_4$ inch
1 cm .... $^1/_2$ inch
1.5 cm .... $^3/_4$ inch
2.5 cm .... 1 inch
5 cm .... 2 inches
7 cm .... 3 inches
10 cm .... 4 inches
12 cm .... 5 inches
15 cm .... 6 inches
18 cm .... 7 inches
20 cm .... 8 inches
23 cm .... 9 inches
25 cm .... 10 inches
28 cm .... 11 inches
30 cm .... 12 inches
33 cm .... 13 inches

Working with different types of oven

All the recipes in this book have been tested in an oven without a fan. If you are using a convection (fan-assisted) oven, lower the temperature setting by 25°F. Convection ovens circulate heat evenly and efficiently around the oven, so there's no need to worry about where to position the baking dish.

Regardless of what type of oven you use you will find each has its idiosyncrasies, so don't stick slavishly to any baking recipe instructions. Make sure you understand how your oven behaves and adjust to that.

Key to Symbols/Nutritional Info

♥   LOW SATURATED FATS
✓   LOW GLYCEMIC (GI) LOAD
WF   WHEAT FREE
GF   GLUTEN FREE
DF   DAIRY FREE
V   VEGETARIAN
Ⓦ   INDULGENCE

          COOKING TIPS, EXTRA INFORMATION,
          AND ALTERNATIVE IDEAS.

Index

First published in Great Britain in 2013 by Conran Octopus Limited,
a part of Octopus Publishing Group,
Endeavour House, 189 Shaftesbury Avenue, London WC2H 8JY
www.octopusbooks.co.uk

An Hachette UK Company
www.hachette.co.uk

Distributed in the US by Hachette Book Group USA
237 Park Avenue, New York NY 10017 USA

Distributed in Canada by Canadian Manda Group
165 Dufferin Street, Toronto, Ontario, Canada M6K 3H6

Publisher: Alison Starling
Senior Editor: Sybella Stephens
Assistant Editor: Stephanie Milner
Art Director: Jonathan Christie
Art Direction, Design and Illustrations: Anita Mangan
Design Assistant: Abigail Read
Photography: Georgia Glynn Smith
Production Manager: Katherine Hockley

ISBN 978 1 84091 633 1

Printed in China

A note from the authors…
Medium eggs should be used unless otherwise stated.
We have endeavored to be as accurate as possible in all the preparation and cooking times listed
in the recipes in this book. However they are an estimate based on our own timings during recipe
testing, and should be taken as a guide only, not as the literal truth. We have also tried to source
all our food facts carefully. However, we are not scientists, so our food facts and nutrition advice
are not absolute. If you feel you require consultation with a nutritionist, consult your family doctor or
healthcare provider for a recommendation.